DAVID O. MCKAY LIBRARY
P9-ELG-359
3 1404 00831 1394

Helpers in Our Community

We Need Pharmacists

by Helen Frost

Consulting Editor: Gail Saunders-Smith, PhD
Consultant: William E. Smith, Pharm.D., MPH, PhD
Executive Associate Dean, School of Pharmacy
Virginia Commonwealth University, Richmond, Virginia

Mankato, Minnesota

Pebble Books are published by Capstone Press
1710 Roe Crest Drive, North Mankato, Minnesota 56003
www.capstonepub.com

Printed in the United States of America in North Mankato, Minnesota.
042012
006702R

Library of Congress Cataloging-in-Publication Data
Frost, Helen.
We need pharmacists / by Helen Frost.
p. cm.—(Helpers in our community)
Includes bibliographical references (p. 23) and index.
Contents: Pharmacists—What pharmacists do—Helping people.
ISBN-13: 978-0-7368-2575-7 (hardcover) ISBN-10: 0-7368-2575-4 (hardcover)
1. Pharmacists—Juvenile literature. [1. Pharmacists. 2. Occupations.]
I. Title. II. Series.
RS122.5.F76 2005
615'.1'092—dc22 2003024241

Note to Parents and Teachers

The Helpers in Our Community series supports national social studies standards for units related to community helpers and their roles. This book describes and illustrates pharmacists. The photographs support early readers in understanding the text. This book also introduces early readers to subject-specific vocabulary words, which are defined in the Glossary section. Early readers may need assistance to read some words and to use the Table of Contents, Glossary, Read More, Internet Sites, and Index/Word List sections of the book.

Table of Contents

PHARMACIST
ROY BROW

Pharmacists

Pharmacists prepare medicines that doctors tell patients to take. They teach people how medicine works.

Genpril
Benylin
Chloraseptic
Fleet
FERROUS SULFATE
bromatap elixir
Goldline
Dimetapp

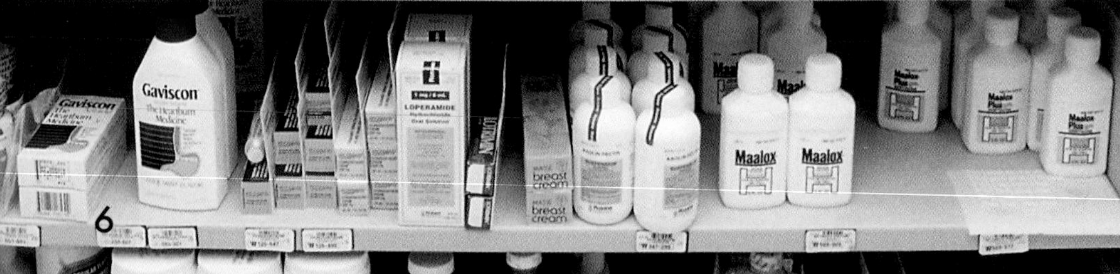
Gaviscon
The Heartburn Medicine
LOPERAMIDE
breast cream
Maalox
Maalox Plus

Some pharmacists work in drugstores or pharmacies.

Mary
Eckhardt
LODOSYN
25 mg

Other pharmacists work in hospitals. They help doctors get medicine for patients.

What Pharmacists Do

Pharmacists keep records on computers. They also read about new medicines.

Pharmacists count pills. They use scales to weigh medicine.

HOWARD

Pharmacists measure
liquid medicine.

Ringers Lactate
1000ml
D5/.33% Saline
1000ml
Dextrose
5% Water
100 ml
Dextrose
5% Water
250ml
0.9% Saline
250ml

Pharmacists put labels on medicine bottles.

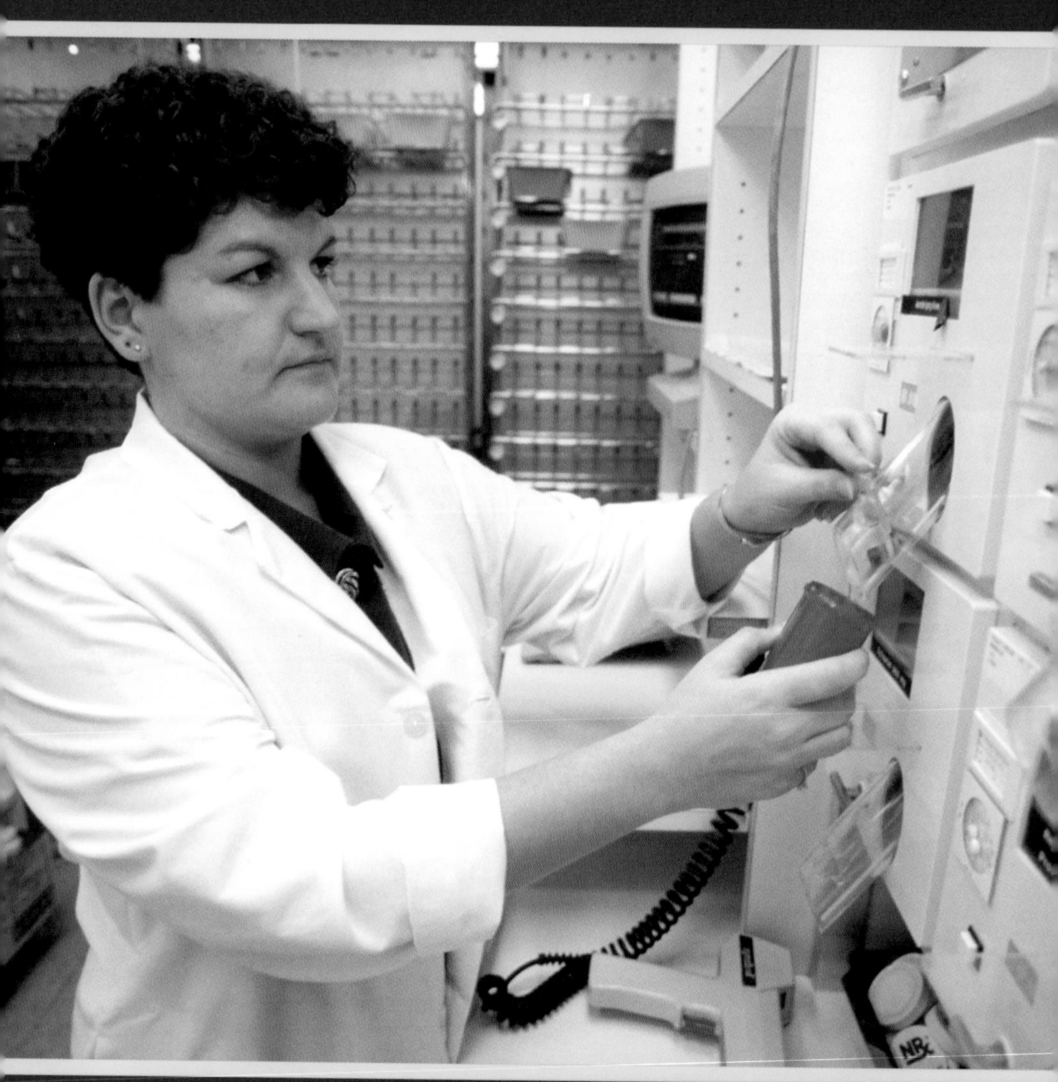

Pharmacists use many machines to help them.

COUGHS & COLDS
Cepacol

Helping People

Pharmacists answer questions about medicine. They help people feel better.

Glossary

liquid—a wet substance that can be poured

medicine—a drug used to treat an illness

patient—someone who receives treatment from a doctor

pharmacy—a store where medicine is sold; some pharmacies are also called drugstores.

pill—a small solid piece of medicine; pills are also called tablets.

prepare—to get something ready

record—a report of facts or information; pharmacists keep records about the medicine people take.

scale—a tool used to weigh something

Read More

Conrad, David. *The Work We Do.* Spyglass Books. Minneapolis: Compass Point Books, 2003.

Gibson, Karen Bush. *Pharmacists.* Community Helpers. Mankato, Minn.: Bridgestone Books, 2001.

Internet Sites

FactHound offers a safe, fun way to find Internet sites related to this book. All of the sites on FactHound have been researched by our staff.

Here's how:

1. Visit *www.facthound.com*
2. Type in this special code **0736825754** for age-appropriate sites. Or enter a search word related to this book for a more general search.
3. Click on the **Fetch It** button.

FactHound will fetch the best sites for you!

Index/Word List

Word Count: 81
Early-Intervention Level: 13

Editorial Credits
Mari C. Schuh, editor; Abby Bradford, Bradford Design, Inc., cover designer; Enoch Peterson, book designer; Wanda Winch, photo researcher; Karen Hieb, product planning editor

Photo Credits
Bruce Coleman Inc./Stephen Ogilvy, 20
Capstone Press/Gary Sundermeyer, 1, 8
Corbis/Leif Skoogfors, 18
David R. Frazier Photolibrary, 14
Folio Inc./Cameron Davidson, 4; Gary Kieffer, 10; Jeff Zaruba, cover; Tom McCarthy Photos, 16
The Image Finders/Mark E. Gibson, 6
Unicorn Stock Photos/Jeff Greenberg, 12

The author thanks the children's library staff at the Allen County Public Library in Fort Wayne, Indiana, for research assistance.